What Our Readers Have Said...

"Although I consider myself a seasoned sales professional, it is helpful to have past learning's refreshed. The books were also beneficial because of the information concerning 'trends' in the sales relationship. The sales process should be viewed as dynamic since business relationships change regularly."

•

"For the particular business I am in and the type of sales calls I have, I find that the books in the Pinpoint Sales Training Series are very often applicable to how I conduct business. I would recommend them to other sales people, just not ones that are in my industry."

•

"These books provide very good concepts. It fits in well with the Bell Leadership training program that I attended in November."

•

"I use this material in these books and apply it to my customers and other employees I work with."

•

"I would like to know other topics. Is there anything on Production Management or Consultative Selling or Time Management?"

•

"These books are great tools that should be used as guidelines for our everyday

supervisory practices. You need to take the time to do a short self-evaluation when reading them."

•

"The Pinpoint Training Series delivers information that could be used in a lot different areas."

•

"I like this because I can take them with me to read at a convenient time. I feel the little time I have to spend in the office is best use on activities that directly relate to revenue opportunities. I like the short amount of time it takes to keep up with these."

•

"I prefer the self-study approach; it fits in with my schedule."

•

"My thought is that the real value of these books comes into effect when doing the action plans."

•

"Short and sweet. These books are easy to comprehend."

•

"I have enjoyed reading these books. They are relevant to today's work environment and the ongoing change in the way we manage our workforce."

•

"I do feel that these books have been very helpful to me at my job."

•

"I think a lot of the recommendations in these books are very useful, and can be applicable to everyday situations. If nothing else, it's a good reference guide to fall back upon if a situation arises in the future."

•

"These books are relevant to today's work environment and the ongoing change in the way we manage our workforce."

•

Diagnosing Customer Needs

Pinpoint Sales Skill Development Training Series

TIMOTHY F. BEDNARZ

MAJORIUM
BUSINESS PRESS

Pinpoint Sales Skill Development Training Series
"Diagnosing Customer Needs"
Timothy F. Bednarz

Graphic design: Monika Pawlak

Majorium Business Press
2025 Main Street
Stevens Point, WI 54481
715.342.1018 • 800.654.4935

ISBN 978-1-882181-83-4

Printed in the United States of America

Introduction

The Pinpoint Sales Skill Development Training Series is designed for targeted training and education regarding increased improvement in a specific skill or competency.

Each book within this series is designed to be easy to use, understand and apply to your job. It can be used as a basis for training individuals, as a discussion guide or as a personal training tool.

Each chapter within this book discusses a specific concept. When you have completed all eight chapters you should have a 360° perspective of the topic.

Additionally, each chapter is divided into specific sections:

- The first section provides you with an overview of the topic
- The Implications section discusses why the concept is important, and why it is important to learn and apply.
- The Strategies, Tips & Techniques to Apply section teaches how to use and apply the particular concept to your work.
- The Points to Ponder section gives you something to think about or to be discussed with a group setting. These are questions not meant to be immediately answered, but to be pondered over time.
- The Training Activity section provides you with the tools to transfer what you have learned to your job. It is designed to help create an action plan to effectively apply the concept.

Each of the topics in this series is time-tested and proven in the marketplace. They have been used by thousands of employees as training tools. Many of the users have commented that what made these books valuable, was the ability to refer to them when a problem surfaced. They indicated that they remembered reading about the exact problem. They referred back to these books and found an appropriate solution.

You will find them equally valuable as a resource in your professional development library.

Table of Contents

LEARNING OBJECTIVES:

- To understand the role of identifying customer needs in selling.
- To understand the consequences of failing to identify customer needs.
- To determine strategies to use to identify customer needs.
- To identify strategies to uncover hidden needs and opportunities.
- To apply customers' needs to effective decision making.

1

Management of Information Assists in Identifying Needs

Salespeople are only as good as the quality of the information they are able to develop regarding their customer's needs. Failure to collect sufficient information and properly identify the customer's needs results in a faulty diagnosis and a poorly crafted solution.

IMPLICATIONS — WHAT THIS MEANS TO YOU

Selling and sales cycles are becoming more sophisticated and complex. As more data is required to determine and analyze a customer's needs, effective salespeople are also effective managers of information. Additionally, increasing numbers of competitors who have access to the average customer through email, the Internet, direct mail and a host of other communication mediums has further complicated the salesperson's job.

Buyers are more sophisticated than ever before, and are aware of their options and the information they must access to make a qualified buying decision.

It is important to appreciate that most sales are won or lost before the initial call on a prospect has even been made. The sale is determined by the salesperson's preparation and his or her application of customer, competitive and product knowledge. As the critical differentiating factor in most sales, the salesperson's experience and expertise in these three key areas is more important than ever before.

STRATEGIES, TIPS & TECHNIQUES TO APPLY

Identifying the customer's needs depends on developing specific information and analyzing it during a needs assessment. Databases can be the salvation for meeting all customer needs.

Most salespeople develop and depend on a database to sell customers. However, many do not collect enough information to completely identify their customer's needs. Salespeople often scribble down notes that contain superfluous information, their databases thus failing to identify the customer's specific needs.

In order to offer a complete picture of the customer's needs, customer databases must be complete and comprehensive. Only at this point can salespeople create a sales approach that is effective and attuned with their customer's needs, concerns and fears. If a customer's database lacks the following elements, it may be ineffective as a dependable sales tool.

Write It Down

Salespeople must get into the habit of writing everything down, no matter how trivial the information may seem. When reviewing the information, it becomes much easier to segment it in order to create patterns and similarities between customers as well as the variables that separate them. This allows salespeople to prioritize their sales efforts with every customer.

Review It Often

Salespeople must frequently update and adjust their databases in a weekly or monthly review. Regularly adding and/or deleting information helps to modify sales approaches according to changing customer needs. This enables salespeople to develop a long-term view of the customer as new needs emerge.

Customer databases should identify the times salespeople need to call or communicate with the customer. As customer contacts are made, databases are updated with the reasons for the contact and the subsequent results.

Identify Your Best Customers

Salespeople can use their databases to identify their best customers and what and when they buy from them. As long-term relationships are developed, salespeople must be able to identify why the customer has remained loyal and use their creativity to transfer that knowledge to the development and acquisition of new customers. A complete and properly managed customer database should provide the salesperson with this key information and highlight how he or she can best meet customers' needs and expectations.

As new customers can have similar needs and profiles, salespeople can use specific information about seasoned accounts to develop favorable relationships with new customers.

Keep the Information Fresh

Customers should be communicated with at least four times a year; how that communication is structured is dependent upon their size and potential. A communication plan needs to be developed to determine the actual method of customer communication. Some customers will require constant face-to-face contact, while others will at times warrant only a phone call.

Customers may also have a preferred method of communication, be it phone, fax or email. Between physical visits, salespeople should use this preferred method of communication.

During ongoing communication customers should be queried as to how their needs may have changed since the last contact. Changing customer needs should be probed with open-ended questions that provide information that completes and updates a customer database. Some areas to probe include:

- Who the customer is currently doing business with
- What bank the customer prefers to do business with
- The things customers are successful in accomplishing and what they are struggling with

- What is falling short of the customer's expectations
- What customers see as current problems and what they fear in the future

Knowing where customers are coming from helps to determine where they are going. To define their future sales potential, salespeople should include this information in their database.

POINTS TO PONDER — SOMETHING TO THINK ABOUT

1. Has technology helped or hindered you in effectively communicating with your customers? How and why?
2. Does your current customer database contain the specific information necessary to thoroughly identify your customers' needs? What other details and information can you add to make it more complete?

TRAINING ACTIVITY — APPLICATION & ACTION PLAN

Determine how a complete customer database enables you to measure your effectiveness.

1. List the data and information required to perform a comprehensive analysis of your customers' needs.
2. Identify the reasons specific information is important to your customer's analysis.
3. Determine how a customer database can be used to cross sell and identify the best prospects for new products.

2

Factors Associated with Identifying Customer Needs

Salespeople often take a simplistic approach to the identification of their customer's needs. They normally focus on one aspect of the business and identify the needs associated with that singular aspect, while ignoring remaining undisclosed needs.

IMPLICATIONS — WHAT THIS MEANS TO YOU

When salespeople take a singular approach to the identification of a customer's needs, they unknowingly shortchange themselves of additional opportunities that a customer may present to them.

This has real implications for salespeople: their efforts to concentrate on a single area or issue while ignoring a host of other potential issues can have them competing in an area inundated by the competition. At the same time there might be additional needs and opportunities where their expertise can be applied.

It is important for salespeople to understand that many customers offer a variety of opportunities at various levels to be taken advantage of. A complete and comprehensive knowledge of the customer, linked with the salesperson's personal knowledge and expertise of various product and service applications, is what ultimately adds value.

STRATEGIES, TIPS & TECHNIQUES TO APPLY

The factors associated with the identification of customer needs will change at every level of the customer's business. These are typically broken into three distinct areas:

The C Level

The C or executive level of selling deals with the senior management of a company. It is described as the C Level because salespeople will be dealing with CEOs, CFOs and CIOs. This is the most difficult level to sell since gatekeepers protect these executives from intrusions on their time and energy. However, the salesperson who is able to breach this level will find a clear field with little or no competition.

The C Level executive's primary concern is results as measured by return on investment, investor satisfaction and market share. A Gallup Study revealed that they are further concerned with costs, customer demands and informational technology.

Additionally, the same study revealed that most C Level executives are not adept at responding to the increasing rate of change. This offers the salesperson an opportunity to assist them in an area in which they admit they are ineffective.

Identifying needs at the C Level means that salespeople must understand and be conversant in the financial terms executives use to evaluate their business. These individuals are not interested in features or benefits, but how a product or service can increase sales and profits.

Core Level

The core levels of a business include manufacturing, operations, marketing, sales, distribution and customer service. At this level all of the specific core functions are closely linked. A problem in one function can cause a chain reaction in all other functions. If one is removed, it can destroy the entire business.

The core level managers are typically vice presidents in charge of a specific function. Like the C Level executive, the core level manager is also interested in results as defined by efficiency, productivity and effectiveness. They typically want to solve problems quickly before there is a chain reaction that can affect other core functions.

Salespeople who wish to understand a customer's business and define their needs should study the core level activities and learn how they are linked. When it comes time to sell to these managers, salespeople can use this information to their advantage. If they can identify the potential chain reaction a specific issue or problem can cause, they can intensify the core level manager's desire to solve it by purchasing a product or service.

Support Level

The support level functions provide assistance to both the C Level and core functions of the business. These include purchasing, legal, training and accounting.

At the support level, many sales are typically transactional, where purchasing agents are shopping for the best value for their money. The term value-added often means price discount to them.

Additionally, purchasing agents may be executing purchasing orders for pre-approved or pre-qualified products and services for both the C Level and core level managers.

At this level, salespeople should stress the price/performance aspects of their products or services as well as availability.

It should be noted the support levels have been most impacted by corporate downsizing. This offers salespeople the opportunity to get to the heart of the business and add value to fill in existing gaps.

Needs Change at Every Level

Salespeople should be aware that the customer's needs change at every level. Typically, the lower the level, the more competition will be encountered. Salespeople have a better opportunity to sell to senior executives if they are able to get in front of them and demonstrate the results and value that can materially impact their business. However, to sell at the higher levels, salespeople should be cognizant that C Level and core level executives are very busy. If salespeople are able to get in front of them, they should be knowledgeable in a host of relevant topics.

POINTS TO PONDER — SOMETHING TO THINK ABOUT

1. At what level do you typically sell your product or service?
2. Do you see other needs and opportunities outside the normal sales contact level at most companies you sell to?

TRAINING ACTIVITY — APPLICATION & ACTION PLAN

Determine how your product or service can specifically help a customer solve their problems and achieve his or her targeted goals.

3

What to Expect When You Uncover a Prospect's Needs

When salespeople uncover their prospect's real needs, they are presented with a wealth of information that most have no idea what to do with. Salespeople know that they have to identify needs, but will typically take one or two favorite facts to build their presentation upon. The rest of the information is ignored or considered inapplicable to the situation.

IMPLICATIONS — WHAT THIS MEANS TO YOU

There is a difference between knowledge and information. Unfortunately most salespeople will collect information about a prospect's needs without converting it into usable knowledge.

When salespeople take the information they have collected and apply their experience and expertise to it, they have the ability to convert it into knowledge that can give them the competitive advantage. This is because most prospects are unaware of the opportunities and possibilities that a company, product or service can provide to them. Indeed, many are completely unaware of their essential product requirements until after the fact.

Salespeople can provide a genuine service to their prospects by the proper application of knowledge and expertise that they can use to make an informed and qualified buying decision.

STRATEGIES, TIPS & TECHNIQUES TO APPLY

Objectives

One of the salesperson's primary goals is to clearly define what a prospect wants to accomplish. It is surprising how many salespeople ignore this basic task and move on to sell what they feel the customer wants and needs.

When salespeople uncover specific customer needs by identifying the changes that the prospect's business is undergoing and the areas of pain and discontent with their existing suppliers, they are ultimately able to identify what the prospect wants to accomplish. A clear identification of customer needs both pinpoints and clarifies what the prospect's objective is.

The common reaction is, "Why don't I just ask what they want to accomplish?" The answer is that until a salesperson takes the time to identify these issues, individual prospects may not know what they want to accomplish, often because they are unaware what is possible or the options available to them.

Requirements

Salespeople must identify the prospect's requirements. These are the items that they "must have" and that drive the need for a solution. If a salesperson is unable to identify these factors, it is unlikely that they will be able to fully satisfy the prospect after the sale.

Since many prospects are unaware of the options available to them and base the majority of their decisions on past experiences, they may not be aware of the requirements they need to receive a fully effective solution and to be fully satisfied with their purchase. Consequently, it is up to the salesperson to discuss the prospect's requirements and identify the elements that they have to have as part of their solution.

Refinement

When salespeople uncover a prospect's needs, they have the ability to refine their objectives and make them more precise. Often prospects are not aware of specific ways that they can improve their operations and effectiveness through the use of the salesperson's products and services.

Every company and product has unique capabilities. Salespeople often fail to leverage these capabilities—which often can solve a number of potential problems—to their advantage.

Salespeople need to focus on the prospect's needs and not their products. In this way they can refine the prospect's need in a manner that creates a need for their unique capabilities. Successfully done, this creates a strong competitive advantage.

Identify Add-Ons

Beyond the prospect's requirements, or "must haves," most have a series of add-ons, or "nice to haves." These are other features and capabilities that they would like to see added to their purchase.

Salespeople must take the time to identify and rank these additional criteria before the prospect has the opportunity to explore other competitors. The success of the sale will depend on how the prospect's criteria are ranked. The salesperson's goal is to create the best match between their product's strengths and the prospect's criteria. The first salesperson in the door has the ability to greatly influence the prospect. Properly done, the competition will find it difficult to compete with the refined and polished criteria.

Compelling Reason

After the salesperson has refined the customer's needs and criteria, it is important to give the prospect a compelling reason to buy their product or service. *Inc. Magazine* reported that one of the major causes of lost sales and failed businesses is the failure to provide prospects with a compelling reason to switch from their existing vendor.

The salesperson who has taken a prospect this far must conclude their analysis with a compelling reason to switch, otherwise they are leaving the door open for a competitor to take advantage of their hard work.

POINTS TO PONDER — SOMETHING TO THINK ABOUT

1. How are you able to apply and use customer knowledge to your advantage?
2. How well do you refine a customer's needs to your competitive advantage?

TRAINING ACTIVITY — APPLICATION & ACTION PLAN

Develop a compelling reason why your prospects should switch from their existing suppliers to you.

1. Start with a rough draft or outline of your reasons.
2. Refine and polish by adding and deleting thoughts and reasons.
3. Create a final draft that is clear and concise.
4. Finalize it into a statement that you can use.

4

Failing to Pay Attention to a Customer's Needs

Many salespeople feel obligated to discuss a customer's needs only because they were taught to do so. The way they sell does not make a clear connection between those needs and their product or service. Rather than paying attention to the customer's needs, they perform a cursory and superficial examination of the needs and quickly forget what was learned.

IMPLICATIONS — WHAT THIS MEANS TO YOU

Many salespeople have been trained on the "sales track" method of selling where they present their product, counter objections, and close the sale. It is estimated that over 75% of salesmen and women are still being training according to this outmoded method of selling. A "comfort zone" for many salespeople, it relies on manipulative sales tactics that many buyers are increasingly resentful of.

The sales track method often ignores the customer's needs and the development of unique solutions to solve their problems and to meet those needs. Because of the number of steps involved, many salespeople are intimidated by a customer focused sales cycle. But for the salesperson interested in building a long-term relationship, the use of a customer focused sales cycle is one of the most effective methods to use to identify the customer's needs and build a solid relationship.

STRATEGIES, TIPS & TECHNIQUES TO APPLY

When salespeople fail to pay attention to specific customer needs, they encounter a number of consequences that are detrimental to their ability to make sales. These include:

Inadequate Customer Knowledge

Salespeople who fail to sufficiently develop information and knowledge of the customer's needs, except on a superficial level, are blindly selling their product or service. Many are more comfortable presenting a product that they feel the customer should be interested in, without any consideration for the customer's needs and problems. These individuals want to sell, not be of service to, the customer. Many experience high levels of rejections because the customer is not interested in what the product can do to meet their specific needs.

An Inability to Develop a Unique Solution

Without sufficient knowledge of the customer needs, salespeople either recommend the wrong product or service or are unable to design a unique solution that matches their product's or service's strengths with the customer's needs.

Some salespeople feel this is unimportant, but unique solutions create product space, differentiate the salesperson and their product from other vendors (thus making it difficult for them to compete), and demonstrate the best value to the customer.

A Lack of Customer Comfort

When salespeople take the time to identify the customer's needs, they are demonstrating care and concern for them. The customer realizes that the salesperson is interested in them succeeding more than they are in making a quick sale. They realize the salesperson who takes the time to understand their business is likely to be around once the sale has been made to resolve any problems and ensure that they are satisfied with his or her purchase. This creates a level of comfort and security for the customer and increases confidence in the salesperson.

Inadequate Rapport and Trust

Customers are naturally suspicious of salespeople. Many have experiences with salesmen and women who have failed to deliver on their promises and disappeared once the sale was made. Many surveys have reported the biggest customer fear is that the salesperson will quickly disappear after the sale.

Salespeople who invest time in developing knowledge of the customer's needs and pay attention to what they are saying build the necessary trust and rapport to develop the relationship and close the sale.

An Inability to Persuade

Without the knowledge of needs and uniquely developed solutions, salespeople have the inability to persuade the customer to buy their product. They often revert to the sales track style of manipulation. This only increases sales resistance and decreases the level of trust required to close the sale. Additionally, after the sale has been made, these salespeople will experience heightened levels of buyer remorse.

An Inability to Create a Sense of Urgency

When salespeople pay attention and identify a customer's needs, they are able to uncover the pain and discontent the customer is experiencing. Only with this knowledge are they able to create a sense of urgency about the need to buy their product or service. A superficial examination of the customer's needs will not accomplish this.

POINTS TO PONDER — SOMETHING TO THINK ABOUT

1. How closely do you link your product or service with a customer's needs and problems?
2. Do you perform an in-depth or only a surface examination of the customer's needs?

TRAINING ACTIVITY — APPLICATION & ACTION PLAN

1. Develop a list of the major accounts you called on during the past year. Identify the accounts where you developed a full understanding of their needs and those where you conducted a cursory examination.
2. Compare and contrast the results you obtained based upon your knowledge of the customer's needs.

5

The Problems and Pitfalls Associated with a Failure to Properly Identify a Customer's Needs

The largest advantage a salesperson has is their mind and the ability to use their creativity to analyze information and develop competitive solutions for their customers. The salesperson who fails to employ their greatest resource is following a path fraught with problems and pitfalls that could easily be avoided.

IMPLICATIONS — WHAT THIS MEANS TO YOU

The sales environment is getting increasingly competitive with a number of sales channels available to customers for information and competitive purchasing of goods and services. While no salesperson is immune to this reality, they do have the largest advantage over all other sales channels. They can use their expertise and experience to develop information, uncover needs and craft unique sales solutions. Most other sales channels are incapable of developing the in-depth understanding of a customer's needs, nor can they build the essential customer relationship. Their primary advantage is price.

Salespeople who understand that they can use their ability to develop personal relationships can gain an advantage. They are able to provide and demonstrate the value most buyers are seeking as well as the expertise they need to be more efficient and productive.

The salesperson who fails to take advantage of this opportunity is squandering the tremendous competitive advantage they have in the marketplace.

STRATEGIES, TIPS & TECHNIQUES TO APPLY

There are several common pitfalls that can be associated with a salesperson's lack of identifying a customer's needs. Salespeople should be cognizant of these and understand their implications.

Product

Many salespeople fail to understand that customers buy products and services to fulfill a need and gain the benefits and value they have to offer.

Companies often offer incentives to sell one product over another, or salespeople have produced excellent results with a specific product or application. Therefore there is a tendency for salespeople to promote a favored product or service based upon their own needs rather than those of the customer.

Undoubtedly, there are times these product recommendations will fulfill a customer's needs, but because they are not linked to their particular needs, there is no interest in them. The customer has not been educated in the specific connection and dismisses the offer.

Price

Price seems to be the major issue most salespeople complain about. They often are informing their company that prices are too high.

When salespeople fail to uncover the customer's needs and craft a unique solution to resolve the customer's pain and discontent with his or her current supplier, they immediately diminish the value of their product or service.

This occurs because the solution is not linked to the customer's needs. If it were, the value of the solution would immediately increase, making price a secondary issue.

Need

Oftentimes customers are unaware of their real needs. They know a problem exists, but may not be familiar with the variety of solutions available to them. Until educated by the salesperson, many do not know how they can increase productivity, efficiency and profitability.

Many customers are working under stressful circumstances, focused on handling daily problems and events. They are often not in touch with their own needs, only because they lack the time and resources to examine their circumstances. A salesperson can act as a consultant when identifying needs because they are sharing previously unavailable expertise that provides insight into their customer's business.

Objections

When customers fail to see the linkages between their needs and a specific product or service, sales resistance will tend to rise. This results in increased barriers, stalls and objections.

As customers perceive a product or service as a means to alleviate their pain and discontent, the value of the solution increases, reducing the stalls, objections and barriers a salesperson might otherwise encounter.

Differentiation

Until salespeople differentiate themselves and their product from the countless other salespeople that call on a customer, they will be considered to be like all of the rest.

The expertise and experience a salesperson brings to the customer is the differentiating factor in sales. Those who leverage these two factors to uncover and identify the customer's needs have the advantage. They have performed a service and demonstrated their value to the customer. This and anything done beyond this point to enhance that value clearly sets them apart from the average salesperson attempting to move their product or service.

POINTS TO PONDER — SOMETHING TO THINK ABOUT

1. Can you identify additional problems and pitfalls that a salesperson can encounter when he or she fails to adequately identify a customer's needs?
2. How have you reacted when you encountered one of these problems and pitfalls? What did you do to recover?

TRAINING ACTIVITY — APPLICATION & ACTION PLAN

1. Create two sales presentations; one based upon your own knowledge of your product or service and one based upon a customer's needs. If need be, use an actual customer to identify the needs.
2. Compare and contrast the two presentations. Identify which is more effective and why.

6

Strategies to Uncover a Customer's Needs

The first step to uncovering a prospect's needs is to sit down and have a conversation with them: not to sell them or present a product or service, but to simply talk about their business. As basic as this seems, it is a very difficult discussion for many salespeople to engage in: it takes time, appears to accomplish little if anything, and keeps them from what they consider to be their primary sales activity.

IMPLICATIONS — WHAT THIS MEANS TO YOU

When salespeople first meet with a prospect, they have a unique opportunity to learn about the customer's business, their environment and all of the elements that define their universe. This requires taking the time to sit down and have a conversation with the prospect—an essential and often overlooked activity.

Failing to engage in such a fact-finding discussion can undermine the rest of the sales process and possibly the sale itself. As this stage provides the first and most significant opportunity to get to personally know the prospect and to get him or her to like them, salespeople should not underestimate its importance.

STRATEGIES, TIPS & TECHNIQUES TO APPLY

When salespeople take the time to have a conversation, several things occur that are critical to the success of the sale:

1. They get the prospect to talk and lower their defenses.
2. They loosen the prospect up to talk more and reveal more about his or her business.
3. They develop trust and rapport.
4. They may discover an item of importance that the competition was unable to find.

The initial conversation should focus on uncovering basic information about the current situation. Salespeople can do this with the use of open-ended questions, which are crucial when trust and perception are critical.

People like to talk about themselves and their business. The more they talk, the more they will like the salesperson and think they are adept conversationalists.

Salespeople will often have difficulty refraining from presenting everything they know about the prospect's business. This puts the prospect on the defensive—people don't like "know-it-alls." Even if the salesperson is correct in everything they say, the prospect will not trust them or want to do business with them.

Thus the customer should be doing all of the talking. Salespeople should apply their knowledge and expertise of the prospect's business to developing open-ended and probing questions.

During this initial discussion, salespeople should avoid discussing the prospect's problems. If salespeople jump prematurely into customer problems, this will immediately place the prospect on the defensive and force them to lie about their current situation. Rather than focus on problems, the salesperson should put the prospect at ease to earn their trust.

When problems are discussed, many salespeople will impatiently focus on the first problem revealed, not allowing the prospect to fully explain the extent of their situation. This is often counterproductive, as research has shown that many prospects will not take action until they air three or more significant problems.

As salespeople continue to ask questions of a prospect, they should use three or four product strengths as the basis of their inquiry. This effectively positions their product or service as a potential solution by making the prospect think that the idea to want those product strengths was their own. The salesperson's job is to create a desire for that which he or she is selling. Open-ended, probing questions built around their product's strengths effectively accomplishes this.

The final aspect of this initial conversation is for the salesperson to create as many options for the prospect as possible. The more alternatives and options that can be created, the greater the salesperson's odds of getting the sale.

POINTS TO PONDER — SOMETHING TO THINK ABOUT

1. What is your initial approach when first meeting with a prospect? Is it a discussion or a presentation?
2. What techniques do you use to get the prospect to talk and lower his or her defenses?

TRAINING ACTIVITY — APPLICATION & ACTION PLAN

1. Identify the three or four greatest strengths that your product offers to your customers.
2. Develop a series of open-ended questions around each specific strength that you can use to develop information while positioning your product or service.

7

Looking for the Pain

Many prospects will admit to problems, needs and concerns; however, most will live with small problems and only fix those they feel are large enough to demand their attention. The problem is that most prospects do not understand the extent of their problems and the consequences of their remaining unsolved. It is the responsibility of the salesperson to protect the prospect from the consequences of their problem.

IMPLICATIONS — WHAT THIS MEANS TO YOU

Salespeople should understand that probing and questioning for pain that pinpoints problems and concerns is not as simple as asking the right sequence of questions. Many customers and prospects don't want to confront their difficulties and deal with them, even if they are pressing. It is psychologically and emotionally difficult to the point many will deny problems even exist.

Most salespeople will immediately back off at the first indication of resistance to this line of questioning. The risk is that telling the prospect that he or she has a problem will immediately cause them to deny the entire problem and shut the sales process down. The key is for salespeople to carefully approach these issues in a manner that does not cause the prospect extreme discomfort, but at the same time gets him or her to both identify and agree that a problem exists.

STRATEGIES, TIPS & TECHNIQUES TO APPLY

Salespeople must get the prospect to acknowledge that they are experiencing a problem. Many prospects won't admit to the scope of the problem out of fear that they are setting themselves up to be sold or will appear negligent not to have taken the time to analyze it.

A common pitfall experienced by most salespeople is that during initial discussions with a prospect, problems and concerns are revealed. The salesperson automatically knows how to fix the problem, and this lures them into a false sense of security as a solution is readily provided to the prospect. However, until the prospect determines the problem is serious enough to fix, there will be scant interest in the salesperson's solution. It's up to the salesperson to analyze the problem and lead the prospect to a logical conclusion: a solution is necessary. This can be effectively accomplished by three questioning or probing sequences:

Identification

Salespeople must be aware that questioning a prospect about his or her areas of pain and discontent can be emotionally disturbing to them. Because many take these as personal admissions of failure, salespeople must tread lightly.

In a study of its customers, Xerox found that they intensely disliked the word "problem," as it comes off as aggressive and pushy. Salespeople should instead use terms such as concern, difficulty, challenge, obstacle and trouble.

Types of questions to use at this stage include:

- What concerns are you experiencing with…?
- What challenges do you have to overcome to…?
- Are there any obstacles to…?

The use of these questions focuses the prospect on their concerns. Salespeople should avoid closed-ended questions at this stage because they force the prospect to make a choice, which is often to avoid the problem. This effectively slams the door on the sale.

Development

The best way for salespeople to develop a problem is to continue to ask questions. Most prospects avoid thinking about problems, hoping they will go away. Most do not examine the potential cost of a problem; otherwise, they would fix them before the solution becomes too expensive.

At this stage prospects have two choices:

1. They can wait for the problem to fester and explode.
2. They can discuss how to avoid the consequences of the problem.

Once a problem has been identified, the salesperson must not allow the prospect to run away from it. They need to develop the problem further.

Some questions to ask at this stage include:

- How often does this problem occur?
- How does it affect you?
- How does ____ respond when this happens?
- How do you feel when this happens?

The more pain a salesperson can develop, the closer the prospect will be to doing something about it.

Consequences

In motivating a prospect to buy when a problem is identified, consequences are more powerful than value. When the prospect is in pain, he or she will do anything to relieve the pain.

Some questions to ask at this stage include:

- What are the consequences if you do not ____?
- What are the repercussions of ____?
- What will be the results if ____?
- What will be the outcome if ____?
- How will this impact your ____?

These three stages will bring the prospect to the logical conclusion to relieve their pain and buy a solution. However, because this series of questioning can be emotionally powerful and painful for the prospect, salespeople must be careful not to put the prospect on the defensive with too many difficult questions. They should carefully observe body language and determine at what stage they may need to back their questioning off.

POINTS TO PONDER — SOMETHING TO THINK ABOUT

1. How carefully have you analyzed prospects' problems before moving the sales process forward?
2. Have you been guilty of presenting a solution before getting a prospect to identify and agree to a problem?

TRAINING ACTIVITY — APPLICATION & ACTION PLAN

1. Develop a series of probing questions that can be used to identify, develop and demonstrate the consequences of a problem in the prospect's mind.
2. Once you have developed these questions, use them at least three times to determine the impact on your sales.

8

Transforming Problems into Needs

Studies have shown that customers buy to solve a problem and not necessarily fulfill a need. Salespeople must use a technique that translates problems into needs while allowing the customer to establish the buying criteria for a solution that closely matches their product's strengths with the customer's needs.

IMPLICATIONS — WHAT THIS MEANS TO YOU

When salespeople successfully probe and discuss a customer's needs, they are actually moving the customer along their own decision making cycle. Properly done, the customer will accept the need for a change and adopt a sense of urgency for identifying and determining the solutions to his or her problem.

This is important for salespeople to understand and grasp because their actions at this stage can affect how or if the sale will occur. The most common pitfall is for an overly anxious salesperson to tell the customer what their needs are and the appropriate solutions. This precludes the customer taking ownership of the solution and could very well undermine the entire sale.

Salespeople are at a critical juncture when it comes time to identify needs and potential solutions. The more they allow the customer to talk at this stage, the more likely they will make the sale. Techniques can be used to encourage and influence the customer, but the idea to take action must be perceived as coming from them and not the salesperson.

STRATEGIES, TIPS & TECHNIQUES TO APPLY

There are three steps salespeople should follow to have their customer identify his or her needs and identify the potential solution. These include:

Have Customer List and Confirm Their Needs

It is presumptuous on the part of salespeople to list the customer's needs. After probing and discussing his or her business, the salesperson may have a complete picture of what the customer needs, but it would be a fatal mistake to tell him or her at this stage.

The idea for change must be firmly implanted in the customer's mind. If the salesperson is to succeed, the customer must have ownership of the solution and perceive that the idea to act was theirs.

The salesperson initially used open-ended questions to probe for the customer's needs. At this stage, he or she should lead the discussion with a series of closed-ended questions. This accomplishes several things:

1. It tests and confirms the information the customer has already provided to the salesperson.
2. It influences the customer's needs and correlates the salesperson's product strengths to the customer's needs.
3. It gets the customer to accept ownership of the idea of change.

Identify Any Additional Needs

Before a salesperson moves the sale forward, they must be certain that no additional needs exist. Typically, once a customer understands the possibility of positive change, additional needs emerge that weren't discussed before.

Salespeople will often find themselves in a situation where it may not be possible to address each of these additional needs. However, it is better to get the complete list of needs in the open now rather than later in the sales process. Many can be dealt with in the third and final step.

Have Customer Prioritize Their Needs

The final step is to allow the customer to prioritize their needs, thus eliminating the guesswork from determining their "hot buttons." Doing so often eliminates many of the needs that the salesperson is unable to address since they become lower priority items.

When salespeople follow this procedure, it eliminates selling a product or service that the customer has little or no interest in. The customer has detailed his or her most important priorities, and this allows the salesperson to sell their product or service in the same sequence.

This procedure has the two additional benefits of allowing the customer to assume ownership of the ultimate solution while making it impossible to stall since they have created a prioritized list of buying criteria that should match the strengths of the products and services being presented by the salesperson.

POINTS TO PONDER — SOMETHING TO THINK ABOUT

1. Do you confirm a customer's needs or do you allow them to identify and confirm their own needs?
2. Do you allow the customer to prioritize their needs?

TRAINING ACTIVITY — APPLICATION & ACTION PLAN

Develop a series of closed-ended questions that will confirm the customer's needs and the information provided to you, influence his or her buying criteria, and allow them to take ownership of the ultimate solution.

About the Author

Timothy F. Bednarz, Ph.D. is CEO of the American Management Development Group, Inc. For over 20 years he has researched, designed and authored hundreds of learning and development programs used by Fortune 1000 companies.

He is also the author of *Great! What Makes Leaders Great. What They Did, How They Did It and What You Can Learn from It* (2011).

Speaking Availability

Timothy F. Bednarz, Ph.D. is available for speaking engagements for your next meeting or association event. He can be contacted at 800-654-4935 or by e-mail at timothy.bednarz@majorium.com.

Bulk Sales

Bulk sales of this book or any other titles available from Majorium Business Press. Inquiries can be directed to sales@majorium.com, or by phone at 800-6654-4935.

Quick Order Form

Fax orders: 715-342-1118. Send this form.

Telephone orders: Call 800-654-4935 toll-free. Have your credit card ready.

Email orders: sales@majorium.com

Postal orders: Majorium Business Press, 2025 Main Street, Stevens Point, WI 54481, USA.

Please send the following books:

____

____

____

____

Please send more FREE information on:

❑Catalog ❑Speaking/Seminars ❑Mailing Lists ❑Consulting

Name: ____

Address: ____

City: ____________________________ State: _____ Zip: __________

Telephone: ____

Email address: ____

Sales tax: Please add 5.5% for products shipped to Wisconsin addresses.

Shipping by air:

United States: $4.00 for first book and $2.00 for each additional product.

International: $9.00 for first book; $5.00 for each additional product (estimate).

Made in the USA
Monee, IL
08 November 2026

67382841R20026